Little Mr. Terrific

Written by Kimberly Bausley
Illustrated by Jefferson Clemons, Jr.
Art Direction by Karen Stiles

Published by IngramSpark™

———

This book is dedicated to some very special people in my
life, who helped me through this journey.

To my husband, Todd,
who is always eager to share funny stories that inspire me.

To Jeff and Netta,
who embarked upon this journey with much enthusiasm
and dedication.

To my daughter, Ashley,
who believes in her mommy.

Tommy usually wakes up early for school but this morning mom had to call him three times before he finally got up.

After Tommy put on his slippers, he brushed his teeth and washed his face.

When he finished in the bathroom,
his school clothes were on his bed.

He put on his clothes, and headed to the kitchen to
have breakfast with his granddad.
Tommy's favorite breakfast was waiting for him,
maple brown sugar oatmeal with toast and orange
juice.
He hoped his mom forgot to put his vitamin on
the table with his breakfast, but it was there, and
Tommy was disappointed.

He does not like to take vitamins.

Tommy's granddad had a vitamin, too, and he felt a little better.

"Granddad, why do we have to take vitamins? They taste so nasty."

"Oh," said granddad, "Didn't you know your vitamins help your body and brain grow healthy and strong?"

"And not only do they
make you healthy
and strong, they give
you special energy
powers to help you
throughout the day,"
granddad added.

"Special energy powers? For real, granddad?!"
"For real, Tommy. Take your vitamin today and see if you have a terrific day."
"Okay," Tommy said softly.

After eating all of his breakfast and taking his vitamin, Tommy put his dishes in the sink and picked up his back pack to leave for school.

On the way to school, Tommy helped his neighbor,
Mrs. Cantera, and her dog, Raisin, across the street.

During the spelling test in school, Tommy knew all of his spelling words.

At recess, Tommy kicked a home
run in kick ball, and his teammates
cheered, calling him terrific!

When school was out,
Tommy played freeze
tag with a group of
boys. He ran fast, so no
one could catch him.

On his way home from
school, Tommy noticed
a baby bird in the yard.
Tommy got the ladder out
of the garage, and climbed
up the tree to put the baby
bird back in the nest.

After saving the baby bird, Tommy cleaned his room...

and finished his homework without granddad reminding him.

At bedtime, granddad was preparing to read
a bedtime story to Tommy. He asked Tommy,
"How did your day go?"
"I had a terrific day, granddad!" and Tommy
told granddad about his day.

When the story was over, granddad said, "Weren't you Little Mr. Terrific, today?! Seems like the vitamin gave you special powers after all."

Kimberly Bausley, native to Dallas, Texas, fell in love with reading books as a young girl. She earned a Bachelor of Arts in Literary Studies at The University of Texas at Dallas. She wrote her first children's book in honor of her husband, who inspired her to capture her dreams, and stirred up her creativity with his own creativity.

Jefferson T. Clemons, Jr., was born and raised in Denver, Colorado. Jeff left Denver to attend Dillard University, where he obtained his Bachelor's Degree in Art Advertising with a minor in business. He spent twelve years in the United States Army, during which time he traveled and started a family with his wife, Vernetta. They have three children and currently live in Colorado. Drawing since he was three, it has always been his dream to be an artist. Although these are his first illustrations for a children's book, he has created numerous logo designs and illustrations, both freehand and digitally.